FRACTURED
THOUGHTS

A COLLECTION OF
POEMS BY:

ROBERT
HUMPHRIES

OKANAGAN
PUBLISHING HOUSE

Published by Okanagan Publishing House, an imprint of Okanagan Publishing Inc:

Okanagan Publishing House
#104 539 Yates Rd
Kelowna, BC, V1V 2T8
www.okanaganpublishinghouse.ca

Printed in the USA, 1st Edition, September 2022

ISBN: 978-1-990389-11-5

10   9   8   7   6   5   4   3   2   1

Library & Archives Canada Cataloguing in Publication
Title: Fractured thoughts / a collection of poems by Robert Humphries.
Names: Humphries, Robert (Robert James), author.
Identifiers: Canadiana (print) 20220282544 | Canadiana (ebook) 20220283230 | ISBN 9781990389115 (softcover) | ISBN 9781990389153 (HTML)
Classification: LCC PS8615.U47 F73 2022 | DDC C811/.6—dc23

OKANAGAN
YOUNG WRITERS'
AWARDS
SHOWCASING THE
NEXT GENERATION

Okanagan Publishing House is a proud supporter of arts and culture in the vibrant communites that line the Okanagan Valley. The **Okanagan Young Writers' Awards** were founded as one way to encourage aspiring writers and nurture the authors of tomorrow.

A portion of the proceeds from this title go directly towards the awards' youth scholarships to inspire their future work. Thank you for helping the **Okanagan Young Writers' Awards** continue "Showcasing the Next Generation of Okanagan Writers."

*To learn more about this exciting initiative and how you can support the **Okanagan Young Writers' Awards**, go to:*

www.OkanaganYoungWriters.ca

Territory Acknowledgement:

Okanagan Publishing House is based in Kelowna and the communities surrounding Okanagan Lake. *"We acknowledge that our business is located on the traditional, ancestral, unceded territory of the Syilx/ Okanagan people."*

To learn more about the Okanagan Nation Alliance and the Syilx people, please visit their website at:

https://www.syilx.org/

TABLE OF CONTENTS

Existential Fret

Loss and Remorse

Imaginative Dalliance

Inspired Events

DEDICATION

*With gratitude to my friend Judy who
would read my poems before I knew
I was writing a book.*

"I have lost the remote to my brain and the channel keeps on flipping,
I need to get some new channels,
I need to find that remote."

- Robert Humphries

EXISTENTIAL FRET

A Life on Fire

Staring out the window I watch the world
go by,
with an ever-present knowledge that it will
slowly die.
The heat escapes my tail pipe rising in the
sky.
Joining billions of other carbon molecules,
invisible to our eyes.

We all know it is up there.
We all know who has put it there.
We all know who will suffer.

Still we speak in vague terms about what
may be.
While others still deny it all together,
speaking instead of jobs and economies.

But we all know it is up there as we watch
our forests burn.
But we all know it is up there as our
children's future blurs.
I watch my daughter smile too young yet to
understand.

— Fractured Thoughts —

I watch my daughter marvel at the world
she may not be able to have.
Still, I am staring out my window watching
the world go by.
Still, I am staring out the window as I feel
the temperature rise.

Alternative Me

Time,
time will tell.

We pick a path,
we pick a truth,
we weigh our options,
then follow through.

Where will it lead?
What are the consequences?
Is this really the truth?

Time,
time will tell.

In the present,
in our own minds,
we speculate,
we try to read the signs.

But what is a sign,
and what is just a rock?

Nothing more,
nothing less.

Rocks could be signs,
omens of the right path.

Or,
It could just be a rock.

Time,
time will tell.

We stumble,
we grasp,
and we hope.

We struggle,
and we fret.

We commit,
and move forward.

Was this the right thing to do?

Time,
time will tell.

We only know what is in front of us,
it is with this alone that we decide.

We take the known facts.
we pick our truth,
we move forward.
Did we miss anything?
Did we miscalculate?

Time,
time will tell.

Those who stand firm,
and declare the only truth,
declare the only path to follow.

Those without doubt,
without regret,
without fear.

Know the least among us.

Uncertainty is a fact,
uncertainty is a truth.

So, look in front of you,
pick a sign,
pick a truth,
and move forward.

Was it the right thing to do?

Time,
time will tell.

Directional Method

Adrift,
rock to rock,
port to port.

Constantly moving.
Looking for consistency,
and finding none.

The path has been murky,
treacherous,
and often intriguing.

There seems to be no clear pattern,
no common theme.

Merely a loose thread,
of timing,
and opportunity.

Each rock,
each port,
has shown promise.
Has appeared to be solid.

But no,
not solid,
not steady.

Instead they have been porous,
left,
vulnerable to the merest wave of change.

One lick,
one lap,
one tide,
sets me adrift again.

Onto the next thing!
Grab onto that next rock,
take shelter in that next port!

For how long?

In a way though,
I have been lucky.
I always seem to land on my feet.

I adapt to the change,
I challenge the new feat.

I have sailed on,
where many would have sunk,
and deplored their condition.
Gotten bitter,
gotten rusty.

Still though,
a little consistency would be nice.
Smoother waters would be welcome,
well earned.

So, I continue to look for that solid lead,
that solid rock,
that solid port.
That takes me to the calm waters of medi-
ocracy.

I do not see it coming,
not in this lifetime it seems.
So, a schemer I continue to be.

Plotting a course,
of,
plan A, B, and C.

Still I remained determined to make one of
these schemes stick,
for one of these rocks to remain solid,
for one of these ports to remain solid,
for my boat not to drift.

But adrift again,
my keel listlessly leads.

Next time my friend,
It will be different,
you will see.

And I will float in the waters,
of a warm and gentle breeze

Forgiveness

Memories,
they are our anchor at sea,
but they drift with the undercurrent.
They move as they please.

Memories,
are loose,
and precariously attached.

They are precious,
and fleeting.

They can flicker away,
like a flame under siege.

They can dance in our minds,
then be snuffed out,
by a breeze.

Memories are what makes us whole,
they hold all our little parts in,
with an ever precarious hold.

They seem as solid as concrete,
thick and unyielding.
Yet when tested,
they prove to be soft and porous,
malleable as a jelly.

How can something so fragile,
and so soft?

Inform our experience,
our feelings,
our thoughts.

How much of ourselves do we only think is
true?
How much of ourselves have we invented,
and forced into that soft goo?

Memories it seems are a complicated mix,
part reality,
part vanity,
part hopefulness.

What is to be learned from a memory's
fluid nature?
Perhaps it is our beliefs that also should not
be so rigid.

For just like a memory our beliefs are not
concrete.
They are porous and soft,
gelatin and incomplete.

— Fractured Thoughts —

When we consider ourselves as a collection
of small pieces;
part reality,
part vanity,
part hopefulness.

Then we begin to see,
begin to understand.
The necessity of forgiveness.

Incomplete Carbon Copies

What if I died today?

What if that truck sped through,
that intersection,
that red light,
and me,
seconds earlier than I was able to break?

What if that was the way it happened?
I did not break in time.

I died today,
and this is just a different version of me,
the other me is dead in the wreckage.

How would I know?

What if life is just a continuation of
moments,
and some of the events that nearly killed us,
actually did?

In that moment we split into two people,
two realities,
one of us dies,
and the other lives on unaware of the
calamity that ensued the other,

— Fractured Thoughts —

Did a version of me die today?
A barrelling chunk of metal going one
hundred and thirty kilometers an hour,
in the form of a truck,
would definitely get the job done.

How many times have I died?

I do not think that I want to know,
for there have been a few close calls.

What if this is the reason I cannot
remember,
large spans.
and events,
of my life?

I have in fact died,
several times,
and not all the memories have transferred,
to the different versions of me.

Do I mourn the death of the different
versions of me?

How would I even do that?

There is an unsettled feeling around me,
perhaps the matter that is now me,
that surrounds me,
is still becoming orientated.

What if I died today?

If I did die today,
then maybe what I feel now,
is the loss of my former self.

Launch Anticipation

Drudgery, drudgery,
sad awful drudgery.

Long periods of boredom,
high intervals of stress.
Mind numbing repetition,
feeling trapped and distressed.

Pinned down by finances,
forced to wait.
Forced to contemplate,
this temporary fate.

So many regrets,
of escapes not taken.
My hole further dug,
into sales jobs frustrations.

Words cannot express,
my heart sorrow sound.
Another phone call,
another shovel in the ground.

Dirt piled high,
Around all the edges.
Threatening to collapse,
and bury me forever.

Escape is in sight,
yet so far away.
I can taste it at night.
I dream of it during the day.
Passionless work,
Empty sensations.
Even the wins feel bitter and tasteless.

The plan has been hatched,
the mechanism drawn.

Just awaiting the time,
to release and take off.

Microcosms

Infinite and fleeting.
Vast yet deceiving.
Sometimes it trickles away,
other times it seems to expand into space.

It is measured,
and readable,
quantified and manageable.
Monetized but not for sale.

Running in a seemingly endless stream,
access is limited and beyond our means.

It is rarely felt when our clocks start fresh,
then monitored and misered as they tick to
the end.

Sometimes it feels like it will never end,
until panic sets in when this delusion is
spent.

Rich or poor.
Strong or weak.
It watches us all,
our secrets it keeps.

As mundane as the air we breath,
it measures our lives from beginning to
end.

Patience

Running,
running,
down we go.

Racing down an uncertain road.

No clear path,
or goal to achieve.

What is behind us is dead,
and what is ahead is unforeseen.

Quicker,
quicker,
our pace exceeds.

We hurdle dangers,
at exalting speeds.

Narrow misses,
that we cannot perceive.

No time to reflect,
no time to take heed.

We move forward at a breakneck pace.

Blindly hurling,
towards a light,
that shifts,
and teases,
just out of sight.

The light dims,
and slides to our right.

Out of reach,
and out of sight.

Darkness creeps around our feet.

Swallows the path,
and halts our feet.

Now where are we?
Our ears are swamped,
by the absence of sound.

No path to follow,
no light to be found.

Stillness now,
no more momentum,
no more obstacles to leap.

No more distractions.

Only the terror of our own heartbeat.

Shifting Certainties

Change is in the air,
again.

I can feel it rustling my bones.

Shifting certainties,
towards the further vague,
and less certain.

It is a magnetic energy,
pulling,
prodding,
me along.

To where?
I do not know.

Change is in the air,
again.

Where it blows,
I will follow.

Straight Lines and Glaring Signs

There are those that say:
there are only straight lines,
straight lines and no signs.

Straight lines that stretch into oblivion.
Oblivion into the past,
oblivion into the future.

No curves,
no detours,
only straight lines.

Life,
death,
in a forever linear form.

There are those that cannot see,
see beyond the lines.

There are those that cannot read,
they cannot read the sharp blaring signs.

They only see the road,
the unblinking stretch.
So that is what they follow.

Why they cannot see,
the dips,
the curves,
the bends,
This I do not know.

Some perhaps,
do not want to see,
and so do not.

Some perhaps,
see,
yet deny.

While others still,
cannot see at all.

I see,
I feel,
I read the signs.

I feel every dip,
every curve,
every bend.

The signs glare at me,
they burn my retinas.

If I fail to act.
If I fail to heed.
If I fail to change my course.

The consequences are on me.

LOSS AND REMORSE

A Thousand Sorrows

"That's too much cheese,"
he said as if to the breeze,
as he coughed and sneezed about the room.

"And Good Lord!
easy on that porridge,
you are stirring it to death!"

He sat with a humph,
and a sigh.
What a grump,
as if he could cook anything at all.

The best he could do,
was scorch a stew,
and burn every piece of toast.

Oh, and his rice…
was not so nice,
it was crunchy and hard to chew.

But he was the man.
Yes, he wore the pants,
everything he said was true.

So, he scrunched up his nose,
criticized in long prose,
as his wife slowly rolled her eyes.

— Fractured Thoughts —

For with out her there,
the cupboards would be bare,
and he would have starved long ago.

She remembered a time,
when he had been kind.
They drank wine,
and spoke of sweet nothings down low.

Before that apple orchard dried up,
dwindled to a shrub,
with hard and prickly thorns.

But alas,
time had passed,
and she herself had grown old,
leaving that wistful optimism behind.

So, as he shoved food into this mouth,
complaining after each swallow,
she did up the dishes alone.

Later that night,
she turned out the light,
and wished him good night,
as he shuffled himself into bed.

He was asleep almost at once,
but her not so much,
her eyes simply would not close.

She stared at the wall,
feeling each tear fall,
and stain her pillow and throw.

Oh what a life,
of mediocracy and strife,
the slow death of a thousand sorrows.

Brief Encounters

Six years ago,
perhaps more,
you took your last breath,
they found you lying on the floor.

A minor car accident,
or so it seemed.
The concussion that followed,
lulled you into a fatal sleep.

You shrugged it off,
for you had been hurt before.
After years of skateboarding,
what was one ache more.

But this was different,
you never knew,
you never guessed.
The consequences blindsided you.

Vividly I remember that day.
Your brother called,
his voice was flat and toneless.

I was stunned,
I had no response to say.

We hung up,
his grim message loomed over me,
I called him back,
and asked what he meant.

He explained again it that same plain way,
and the reality settled in,
you had indeed passed away.

What followed was a period of time,
where sobriety was not an option.
I lived in a cloud of smoke too deep for my
grief to penetrate.

This went on,
I am not sure how long.

Time passed,
your funeral passed,
and I moved on,
or so I thought.

Then the dreams began.

I am not a sentimental man,
nor do I believe in a heaven above,
nor a hell below.

But I somehow feel that you are not done
with me.

— Fractured Thoughts —

You beckon me from far away,
or from close by,
it is hard to tell.

Distances get smudged,
you are far,
yet close,
yet ever present in my dreams.

We hang out,
like before,
doing ordinary things.

There are times when you are right next to
me,
and others where you are a vague third
party,
not part of the action,
more observing what ever bizarre scenario
I have created.

It makes me question the permanent nature
of death.

Most vivid was the dream where you came
back to life,
others had gathered around you,
but I could tell that something was not
right.
The people around you were melting slowly
into the floor,
slouching downwards,
as if everything around you was corrupted
by death.

Your mum had heard that you were there,
she was crying,
she was running towards you.

I stepped back,
I so badly wanted to step forward,
but after all you cannot cheat the rules of
nature.

I told you to stop,
I told you to leave,
I turned,
I left the room and shut the door.

When your mum arrived,
she burst through the door,
and you were gone.

— Fractured Thoughts —

You had listened,
you had heeded my warning,
as you had before.

You left them alone to grieve.
Your presence is softer now,
but you have not left me.
You linger in my strange dreamscapes,
sometimes talking to me,
and sometimes not.

That is okay,
it is hard,
but that is okay.

I am not saying move on,
I enjoy our brief encounters.

My dreams must be entertaining enough to
keep you coming back,
perhaps a diversion from whatever you are
experiencing.

The door is open my friend.

Continue to come on by,
until you feel that you can move on.
Your company is sorely missed.

You are the most real person that I have
ever known,
you always told it straight,
with no apologies.

You are missed.
So, if you are feeling restless,
or need a laugh,
come on by.

A brief encounter,
a tall moment,
the door is always open.

Summer's End

The water park is silent,
it splashes excited children no more.

The entrances have chains,
and the pavement is dry.

There is a subtle chill that occupies the
morning hours,
just enough to make one consider wearing,
long pants.

Summer is over.

Once vibrant leaves have begun to wither,
and float to the ground.

There have been heat waves,
of extreme discomfort,
devastating fires,
and a wave of pandemic.

Still,
I hate to see Summer go.

Still,
I miss my increasing former,
favourite season.

Fires,
extreme heat,
and work stress,
are deteriorating my childhood memories.

The winds of change are upon us.

Summer means something different now,
youthful innocence is wearing thin.

Replaced with worry,
anxiety,
and fear of the unknown.

What will next Summer bring?
More drought?
More fire?
More dread?

I cling to the Summers of my youth,
when the heat,
meant fun,
and swimming.

What will the Summers of my daughter
mean?

More sun,
less fun,
more danger?

I hold onto hope,
I hold onto Summer,
I hold onto the Summers of better days.

Silence

The noise!
The noise!
Egads the noise!

The delicate bird tries to shout,
tries to shout over the assault,
the bustle,
of human activity.

Engines rev,
horns blare,
phones ring,
drowning out the natural world.

The bird's frantic chirp,
is no match,
is no contest,
for the cacophony of human noise.

On this spot there was a meadow,
on this spot there was a stream,
on this spot there was serenity,
now shattered by the cumulation of the
human scream.

— Fractured Thoughts —

What will happen,
when the last gentle bird call dies out?
When all that is left,
is humanities obnoxious belch?

Sadly, if that day does come,
then eventually our own sounds will also
grind to a halt.

For once the birds have ceased to chirp.

Humanity will also,
slowly fall,
silent.

Closed Doors

Mistakes were made,
opportunities were lost.

There was that time when I turned down
that job.
There was that time when I should have
turned down that job.
There was that time when I should have
walked away but stayed instead.

There were fits of rage,
and tempers lost.

There were times when compromise was
needed,
but I would not bend.
There were times when action was need,
but I lingered instead.

There were times when I should have held
my tongue,
my temper caught up with me.
I lashed out at the ones I loved.

I am not perfect,
I have never pretended to be,
yet still the cobwebs of my failures bother
me.

— *Fractured Thoughts* —

They creep up when I am not looking and
linger on my mind,
dangling the future that I left behind.

But that time has passed,
that opportunity gone.
I can only move forward,
but I still feel the loss.

It is that unknown loss that still bothers me.
That unsung song,
would it have been a sweet one?
Or a horror that I dodged?

I will never know.
No one ever knows.

So, what do I do with this unknown loss?
This shapeless pain that bothers my
thoughts.

I would like to think that it will fade away.
It will dissipate like a cloud after a morning
rain.

Yet this seems unlikely,
too good to be true.
The truth is more unsavory,
less clean and more stained with mildew.

It seems more likely that a tiny part will
remain.
Lay dormant and forgotten,
but still felt in some small way.

I look forward as always,
and put on a brave face.

Mistakes were made,
opportunities were lost,
now I must learn from the pain.

Childhood Roads

From my childhood home to my friend
Peter Schalke's house,
there are four ways to get there by foot.
Each of the four ways have variations,
that take shorter or longer.

Some are side roads with small forest paths
in between them,
some are long forest paths shaded from the
sun.

The most direct route is along the train
tracks,
full heat,
no shade,
this is the quickest route.

I used to walk everywhere.

Sure, I could have taken a bus,
but that was boring,
and required waiting.

Walking took longer,
yet there was no stillness,
no waiting.

The constant motion forward soothed me,
as if I was leaving my cares behind,
one footstep at a time.

Now I drive,
now I wait.
The stillness consumes me.

I drive for work,
long distances,
that take me towns apart.

Yes, I am still moving,
but it is not the same.

I move now with a purpose,
a mission,
a goal.

The idle,
carefree movement,
of my childhood is gone.

No amount of money will regain it.

The adult world does not allow for such
freedom,
such nonchalance movement.

— Fractured Thoughts —

Even adult recreation has a purpose,
has a goal.

The goal is to have fun.

Try to explain this goal to a child,
the puzzlement on their face,
they do not understand.

And why should they?
What a ridiculous goal,
such a goal only exposes the nature of adult
activity.

To be productive,
to be industrious,
to make money.

I long for that puzzlement,
I wish that I did not understand,
but I do,
and nothing can change that.

I can only dally,
In childhood amusements,
I can no longer live there.

I have been evicted from my childhood,
through sorrow,
through duty,
through my own eagerness to grow up.

From my childhood home to my friend
Peter Schalke's house,
There are four ways to get there by foot,
and before I die,
I would like to walk them again.

IMAGINATIVE DALLIANCE

Avoidance

A stillness settles in.
A muffled silence where you can feel each
breath.
In and out heaves my chest,
while the air around me seems to condense.

The putrid silence absorbs the air,
stifling the movement of the tiniest hair.
Nothing moves.
Nothing dares.
In that terrible careless stare.

A Frigidity so deep, so dense.
Cast my way with a flicker of contempt.

It holds me there,
my feet held fast
Unable to flee from its icy grasp.

One second,
two seconds,
three seconds gone.

Before I break eye contact,
my eyes shuffling to the ground.
Her gaze now broken my feet begin to
move.

— Fractured Thoughts —

I slowly scurry past her,
feeling the universe again begin to move.
With her three feet behind me now my
pace quickens.
I reach the exit and escape her prison.

The most beautiful women I have ever seen,
with eyes so cold I thought my lungs would
freeze.

Mopping the Sea

Jim Brown stood at six foot two,
his shoulders were broad and strong,
he had a shock of red hair,
and wore a steadfast glare,
as he stared at the seashore below.

"What a mess,"
he cursed under his breath,
as he watched the brine come and go.

"This will not do,"
he blurted to his shoe,
as he stomped on a nearby shell.

With an iron grip,
he grabbed his mop and bucket,
then stormed down to the beach below.

"I'll clean this all up, the seaweed and
froth!"
He bellowed at the top of his lungs.

Slapping down his bucket,
he wrung out his mop,
and pointed it menacingly at the sea.

Then he got down to work,
scrubbing the sand and the dirt,
cleaning the rocks,
and rinsing the logs.

The tide rolled away,
revealing more sand to save,
from the scourge of the salty water.

He worked tirelessly all day,
scrubbing away,
never stopping,
never relenting.

As the sun faded away,
with the turf kept at bay,
he raised his mop in victory.

"And stay away!"
He hollered across the bay,
then finally slumped and rested.

Soaked in sweat,
tired and wet,
he turned to walk back to shore.

Only to hear,
a horror creeping nearby,
the lapping of a moist and salty hand.

For the sea never stops,
never rests,
never relents to a mop.

His great shoulders sagged,
his crimson hair limp and drag,
his knees turned to jelly.

The sea was coming back,
violent and fast,
washing away all his careful progress.

All his clean rocks,
his sand,
his dirt,
his logs,
once free of the vile brine.

Now all washed away,
coated in the salty spray,
moved from their places of perfection.

Jim Brown never heard himself scream,
as the waves soaked his knees,
while he feebly wielding his mop against
the turf.

He barely saw the behemoth wave,
crash down on his face,
rattling is head to and fro.

— Fractured Thoughts —

He only vaguely felt the grip,
of the undertow's icy breath,
as it yanked his legs from beneath him.

As the briny liquid filled his lungs,
a flash of consciousness,
a revelation,
a final thought.

No mop,
no man,
can tame the chaos of the sea.

One Speckled Rock

The arid air dries my skin.
irritates my eyes,
and chaps my lips.

Moisture absorbed from my every pour.
the cold crisp air,
violates my skin.

My breath billows in front of my face,
as I hesitantly gaze upon the pond ice.

One tentative step,
one cautious push,
I stop and listen,
for danger underfoot.

The sound of dripping water somewhere
out of sight,
the howl of the wind,
but no cracking of the ice.

Another step,
a cautious hop,
the path seems clear,
so I plod on.

— Fractured Thoughts —

One after the other,
my feet shuffle forward,
ever so careful,
across the precarious pond.

My goal is clear,
the object near,
the speckled rock,
I need to hold dear.

Why I need this speckled rock,
I will never know,
but this speckled rock,
I simply must hold.

Inching forward,
step by careful step,
so close now,
I can feel my breath.

One step closer,
an audible crack!
The ice is shifting,
No!
This cannot be how this ends.

This speckled rock,
must be mine,
its very essence screams of the divine.
I stand my ground,
strengthen my nerve,
and boldly move two more inches near.

Another crack!
Louder this time,
one more step forward and I could plunge
through the ice.

I pause to consider,
my next crucial move.
Do I risk moving forward?
Or do I retreat to shore?

"Neither," I say,
to the speckled rock close at hand.
"I have come this far,"
so I steady myself and contemplate.

A lightening of thought,
a brilliant scheme!
I slip off my jacket,
and hold it by the sleeve.

With a brash motion,
I fling my jacket out,
aiming the hood at the speckled rock.

— Fractured Thoughts —

I miss,
but carry on,
in a persistent fever,
swinging my jacket passionately at my
treasure.

One time,
two times,
just one time more!

My jacket hood encapsulates the speckled
rock.

My heart pounds,
my body aches,
the cold setting in against my chest.

Gingerly I pull on the fringe of my jacket
sleeve.
The progress is slow,
but with every inch the speckled rock
moves my heart sings.

I can hear the speckled rock roll softly on
the ice,
I can hear the ice creak,
and crackle from under my weight.

Which will give first,
my nerve?
Or the ice?

I harden my stare on my jacket hood,
and ignore the imminent breaking ice.
I am staring so hard,
I almost do not see,
that I have pulled the speckled rock right to
my feet.

I did it!
I have it!
The speckled rock is all mine!

I hold the speckled rock high in the air,
like it is a star that has dropped from the
sky.

My triumphant moment is rudely
interrupted,
by a decisive boom.
The ice around me is beginning to shatter,
like a thousand crystal tombs.

Panic breaks my trance and I leap
backwards into the air,
I land flat on my back,
and gasp for air.

— Fractured Thoughts —

Like a penguin,
I slide toward the shore.
My jacket trailing behind me in one hand,
the speckled rock firmly clenched,
in my other hand,
leading the charge.

By some miracle,
some lucky twist of fate,
I manage to slide to shore,
before the pond ice shatters into a million
jagged pieces or more.

Could I have perished?
Could my life have abruptly ended
there?
Sure,
maybe,
but I have my speckled rock,
and what is life without a little flair.

·

The Fish are Biting Tonight

Rosemary sits at the edge of the pond,
watching the ripples expand from where
her rock fell.
The dull grey water has an oily sheen.
No frogs are croaking tonight,
even the insects lay still and unseen.

She lulls one foot into the dull oily mass,
and teases with the idea of going further
than that.
Water that no insect dares to swim,
certainly not even fit for a whole human
limb.

She fiddles and frets,
twisting her thumbs,
staring with abandon at the action that may
come.

So fixated on that possibility she does not
notice the water stir,
curl around her foot,
then sink its teeth into her middle toe.

Her trance instantly broken she yanks back
her foot.
Droplets of blood sit on top of the water,
then sink down to the mud.

Her breath becomes ragged and her body
begins to move.
She slowly retreats from the water almost
expecting the whole ground to move.

Her pupils sharpen,
her wits return,
as she hustles away from the oily murk.

The water settles,
once again flat and lifeless.
It shines in the moonlight.
Reflecting the stars above.

Time to Go

Afternoon tea is simply the best.
Unless of course,
you have a quarrelsome and bothersome
guest.

He used all my sugar,
he spilled my good cream,
he sullied my fine linen,
when he wiped his greedy teeth.

Such manners,
I say!
Who raised this person up?

Who taught him it was okay,
to behave as such?

And the conversation!
Good lord!
The things that he says!
Blabbering on about ridiculous and
outrageous hearsay.

Halfway through that long and droll
afternoon,
I had the hideous feeling that he would
never leave.
That I would be stuck here forever,

listening to the verbal diarrhea of this
obnoxious galoot.

I fought and I fought,
the most discourteous urges as I squirmed
in my chair.
Oh, how good it would have feel to shove
that last scrumpet,
right up his nose,
and dump my last dregs of tea in his hair.

For that would surely make him shut up!
He would spitter and spatter,
then leave in a huff.

But no,
not I,
my courtesy runs too deep.

Engrained into me by my mother,
along with my sister and brother.

At last my salvation!
A trill of a phone!
Whatever they are selling I will buy two
dozen,
if not more.

With a graceful nod,
I usher him out of the room.
On the pretext that some grand emergency
has just bloomed.

"So sorry my friend we will have to do this
again soon."
That is of course if he can find me,
when I move to the moon.

With a gentle click of a door,
and the twist of a lock.

I suddenly realize,
who the hell was that man anyways?

INSPIRED
EVENTS

Destination

My wheels go faster,
round and round.

My legs,
pump,
and pump,
gliding over the ground.

I take the corner,
and pedal through.
Pushing,
pushing,
to somewhere new.

Complete focus,
of my wheels on the ground.
Constantly scanning,
picking my path.

Heart pumping,
legs aching,
but I cannot stop now.

Almost there,
one more hill.

— Fractured Thoughts —

Pushing,
pushing,
my breath pants loud.

I crest the hill,
I glide down.
The air is whipping,
my heartbeat levels out.

Out of the sun,
and into the shade,
clear cold water,
greets my face.

Slowly,
surely,
my heartbeat slows down.

In the frigid water,
my skin burns,
I sink,
I am found.

Diving down to the bottom deep,
I am home again,

Here,
I am complete.

The Darker Side of the Coin

I despise this world,
and how we live.

We struggle,
and fight for material things.

Money brings me no happiness.

Money dogs me,
drives me,
pushes me to sickness.

All the great deeds.
big breakthroughs,
historical moments.

They boil down to money,
and the need to acquire it.

When I have it I feel nothing,
when I do not have it I feel miserable.

The stress of being poor,
the stress of being rich,
the stress of money.

— Fractured Thoughts —

Money drives our entire human world,
it is the means,
and the goal of our existence.

Those who have it,
will do anything to keep it.

Those who do not have it,
will do anything to get it.

Entire revolutions have been fought over
money.

Strip away the ideals,
the rhetoric,
and all that is left is money,
who has it and who wants it.

The poor are tired of being poor,
so they murder the rich.

The rich are scared of being poor,
so they live in fear,
and murder the poor.

Murder,
blood,
money.

Money is not even real,
it is a creation of our own greed.
Our need to stand taller,
to be better,
than those next to us.

We have made it a necessity,
a cruel requirement for existence.

A requirement that I feel every day.

When I meet the requirement,
I do not really care.

When I fail to meet the requirement,
I feel only despair.

I am hyper aware of the lean,
that money has on my life.

I also see the other side of the coin.
I see the terrible desperation,
festering in those who have no place to rest
their weary feet.

It scares me,
so I play along,
I behave.

But,
if I had one wish,
one magical,
unforeseeable truth.

I would turn this world upside down,
I would upheave,
I would expel,
this so called normal.

Poor,
rich,
would all fall on their face's,
and rise again,
to something better.

But,
I see the desperation,
the fear,
the uncertainty,
of those without money.

And it scares me.

So I behave,
I fall in line,
and collect my pay.

Freedom

What is the goal of society?

To strike a balance between,
responsibility,
and individual needs?

The responsibility,
to do the right thing,
for the greater good.

Why should you consider the greater good
at all?

The "We" of society,
has become watered down.
Drowned in individual wants,
and greed.

Is this not the reason society is falling
apart?

Those who cling to their freedom,
in the face of absurdity,
have forgotten the "We",
they have forgotten the greater good.

I have not forgotten,
I have not forgotten the greater good.

— Fractured Thoughts —

Together we stand,
divided we fall.

We are falling,
every day,
inch by inch,
towards chaos,
in the name of freedom.

We are free,
free to fall,
free to infect others,
with our ignorance.

With our ears shut,
we shout,
we scream,
about our freedoms,
and the forces that threaten to take them
away.

On deaf ears are the pleas for,
rational thought,
consideration for others,
for the greater good,
lost.

Society unglues,
one person,
one irrational call for freedom,
at a time.
Like so many societies before us,
we are coming undone.

One cry for freedom,
one grab for more,

from those who already have so much,
deteriate the greater good.

Society will not perish from tyranny,
nor oppression.

Society will perish under the banner of
freedom,
as the greater good,
once again evaporates from the human
consciousness.

We will fall,
waving the banner of freedom to our last,
ragged breath.

Red Waves

Rage is hard to quell.

Rage boils and burns,
it churns in my guts,
it rises up my throat,
and spews from my tongue.

Despite myself,
I feel it rise,
like a fire,
freshly fed,
roaring to life.

Perhaps,
It was never truly out?

Perhaps, it burns like an eternal ember?
Waiting for the kindling,
to end its drought.

The moment arrives,
the fuel trickles down,
and the blaze rages up.

Regret,
always regret,
lingers when the flames simmer out.

Regret for what I said,
what I did,
for the fear I installed in those I love.

The torrent of flames,
trickles back down,
but the ember remains.

Then regret,
deep seeded regret.

Rage is hard to quell.

Sometimes it is called for,
the world is not a just place.

More often than not,
rage only makes a situation worse.

No true justice is brought by a raging mob.

The mob fights,
and thrashes,
and kills.

This kind of violence cannot be sustained.
Ultimately the wave dies down,
crashes to the ground,
leaving pain and confusion in its aftermath.

Rage is hard to quell,
rage must be quelled,
if long term change is be achieved.

Regret,
bitter,
acidic,
regret.

Tomorrow is a new day.

Rage is hard to quell,
rage must be quelled,
if true progress is to be made.

Salt Water Yearnings

I miss the ocean.

On a distant shore,
the waves play,
and foam to the rhythm of the tide.

I miss the salt,
the way it licks your skin,
covering you head to toe.

I miss the roar of its arrival,
and the quiet,
of its retreat.

Dangerous and life giving,
the dichotomy of our own fragile existence.

I miss the assurance,
the constant flow of water.

I miss the ocean.

Eleven long years ago,
I moved inwards searching for a more
prosperous tide.

— Fractured Thoughts —

I found love,
I found sunshine,
I found a second chance at balance.

And still I yearn,
subtle,
yet constant

Yearning will sneak up on me at the best of
times,
and it will nag at me at the worst of times.

When will I return,
to the bubble,
and turmoil of the sea?

When will the time be right?

For today I ride a different tide,
one of obligation and opportunity.

When will that tide usher me home?

I wait,
I feel,
I long.

Someday the current of life will bring me
home,

back to the sloshing,
slushing,
salt of my childhood.

Someday,
until then I dream,
long,
and yearn,
for the salt water again.

Small Sacrifices

Get up,
shower,
eat breakfast.

Start the car,
battle traffic,
get coffee.

Wake up,
and evaluate.
What needs to be done today?

Prioritize,
plan,
finish coffee,
get started.

Complete my tasks,
make my asks,
then race back to you.

To be there on time,
to see you smile,
through the school gates.

Mindless chatter,
on the way back home.
Then to the matter,
of what to eat.

Cook dinner,
do the dishes,
then bath time and more play.

Stories and teeth brushing.

A million hugs and kisses later,
and late to bed again.

Tired and sore,
my mind melts to the floor,
as I stare at the ceiling.

I haul myself up,
climb the stairs,
and wash up for bed.

Then drift into a slumber.

Six a.m. again,
on my feet,
and down the stairs.
For our prework cuddle.

— Fractured Thoughts —

I love you and goodbyes,
your warmth clings to my stride,
as I walk out the door again.

Back out into the world,
where money makes me work,
to provide a better life for you.

I wish this were not the way,
but this world I cannot change,
it possesses a force greater than you and me.

This sacrifice I gladly make,
to ensure that you are well and safe,
still free to live in your own little world.

That bubble I will maintain,
so your spirit does not have to change,
and conform to the casual harshness of this
world.

This I do for you,
with no complaint,
or regret.

For this is how much I love you.

Small sacrifices need to be made,
for a price is always paid.

This is a price I will gladly pay for you.

Patterns of Life

A Blue Ukulele,
nothing more.

Plain to the sight,
yet rich to the ear.

Transformative,
in every way.

Strumming and fretting,
strumming and fretting,
so far no more.

I cannot even play a song yet,
still,
I am in love.

An hour can go by,
the world can go by,
it does not matter.

Strumming and fretting,
strumming and fretting,
pure joy.

There are songs in my head,
that are aching to get out.

— Fractured Thoughts —

Not yet,
I am not ready.

Must practice my technique,
must learn the chords,
must learn my own rhythm.

Strumming and fretting,
strumming and fretting.

Already I can sense the rhythm,
the variety,
the swagger,
resonating from four simple chords.

Already I can sense,
the patterns of life.

Strumming and fretting,
strumming and fretting.

How can such complexity,
such joy,
come from four simple chords?

G
C
E
A

G
C
E
A

G
C
E
A

Strumming and fretting,
strumming and fretting.

— *Fractured Thoughts* —

Love Bends

Love,
what are its boundaries?

Some say that,
love is unconditional.

I disagree.

All relationships,
emotions,
devotions,
have conditions,
and boundaries.

Love is no different,
it does not stand alone.

Love can be eroded,
neglected,
abused,
and slowly day by day,
it can fade.

Even the proposed,
unconditional love,
of a parent for a child,
can be eroded by constant daily struggle.

Nothing is so sacred,
that it cannot disappear.

So where am I in this process?
How intact is my parental love?

It is not gone,
but it is damaged.

The limits of my parental love,
are currently being tested.

I would like to say,
that my love for my daughter,
is eternal.

However,
this is simply not true.

Already I can feel it slide,
waiver,
and erode.

Daily fights,
arguments,
and lack of rest,
are accumulating on my mind.

It was small at first,
inconsequential.

— Fractured Thoughts —

Today,
today, however,
the negative balance is strongly felt.

The ground beneath my love for her,
has shifted.

Cracks,
fissures,
have revealed themselves,
in the sand,
that I once thought to be concrete.

Indifference towards her,
has risen towards the surface.

So where do I go from here?
Now that,
the fissures of indifference,
can no longer be denied.

What now?

Are these the winds of change,
that rattle my bones?

Can it ever go back to the way it was?
Before,
the ground was tested.

Or will my love for her,
forever,
have an edge?

A traumatic jagged point,
waiting underneath,
the increasing thin veneer of my fatherly
devotion.

I do not know,
but I fear that,
irreversible damage has been done.

Love has boundaries,
conditions,
and perhaps,
mine has begun to break.

And then,
something unexpected happens.

A calm,
a peace,
a return to the days of old.

There is still sand beneath my love for her,
but now,
kindness rises to the surface instead.

— Fractured Thoughts —

A golden light,
a minor repair.

It would seem,
that what I perceived to be breaking,
was merely bent.

What is bent,
can be mended.

Perhaps,
that is how love works.

Love is a balance,
a sliding scale of grey,
not an exercise in absolutes.

So, I bask in this moment,
this golden light
and hold it tightly.

Going forward today,
I will always try to remember.

That in love,
there is always,
a shimmer of light,
in the deepest of dark moments.

That shimmer of light is more powerful,
more significant,
more potent,
than the deepest dark that surrounds it.

Gasoline Fire Love

There have been highs,
and there have been lows.

There have been moments of ecstasy,
and there have been low blows.

Our love has not been perfect,
as I have already said,
there is no perfect time for us to move
ahead.

A clear path to happiness we have not
known.
There have been dead ends,
mistakes,
and too many times our love has drained
low.

To say it has been easy,
it is plain to see,
neither of us choose the easy path,
easy is not in our genes.

If you are stubborn,
then I am truly an ass,
but know this my love I will always have
your back.

I will always defend you,
as you will always defend me.

I will offer my hand,
when you have fallen to your knees.

Our love is not a flame that flickers in the
wind,
it is a gasoline fire,
that occasionally grows dim.

That is not say that it does not come
roaring back to life,
our love is more durable than a flimsy
romantic light.

There was that time we fought bitterly
before you went to work,
the reason why I am no longer sure.

All the same I insisted in an angry tone,
"take your lunch or you will be hungry
when you get home!"

Even at our worst we still deeply care,
we may scream and yell,
but at least we clear the air.

— Fractured Thoughts —

You will always know where I stand,
whether you like it or not,
and right now I stand next to you,
and our love.

I love you deeply,
you know this to be true.

Through good times,
and bad times,
our love is renewed.

Lover's Gamble

Some speak of love as unbreakable chain,
strong,
taught,
each link secure in its claim.

Some speak of love as an everlasting flame,
nor wind,
nor water,
can extinguish its blaze.

I know however that love is not so,
links can break,
flames easily tamed.

If love is a chain,
it is a brittle one.
If love is a flame,
it is vulnerable to an amble breeze.

Love like all things is a living being,
susceptible to neglect,
starvation,
and fear.

A love not paid attention to,
fed,
and calmed,
will wither and die.

— Fractured Thoughts —

The chain will shatter,
the flame will be snuffed out.

Love after all is not a static thing.
Once it has been created,
it continues to change.

It changes with the hearts and minds,
of those who share it.

Sometimes those hearts and minds change
too drastically,
they drift apart,
and their shared love fades away.

Sometimes those hearts and minds meet a
violent event,
their love is ruptured,
and that love bleeds out.

And sometimes those hearts and minds
endure,
they grow together,
and their love perseveres.

However, love ends,
or adapts.

Know this,
love will be tested.

Obstacles will be presented,
temptations laid bare,
weaknesses exploited,
a grave threat will always be near.

Love must be nurtured,
well fed,
and calmed.

Love must be allowed to grow,
and possibly move on.

And despite your best intentions,
love still might slip past you.
It can grow too big to handle,
or shrink too small to hold onto.

For love is a fickle thing,
it can envelope you today,
and evaporate tomorrow.

Be kind to your love,
and it may stay.
Accept it,
cherish it,
whatever path it may take.

— Fractured Thoughts —

Be like the grass in the wind swept field,
and allow your love to freely swarm around
you.
Your love may stay,
or it may flutter away.

For chains break,
And flames blow out.

When changes come about.

Time to Get Some Sleep

Am I a reluctant father?
Could I walk away,
from my daughter?

Do I feel trapped?

It hurts to think this way,
but fatherhood lately,
is a push.

Am I just run down,
and frustrated?

Maybe.

I love my daughter with all my heart,
but I also have dreams,
and ambitions.

I pursue these dreams late at night,
when no one demands,
my time.

By then,
so much energy,
has already been spent,
there is so little left for me.

— Fractured Thoughts —

Is it selfish to have ambitions beyond my
family?
I do not think so.

Then an emergency,
my phone rings,
and beeps at me.

My daughter is missing from school,
and my heart races.

In the end,
it is a false alarm,
the panic however,
was not.

Perhaps what I need is a proper balance?

Where my ambition,
and family can both benefit.

Perhaps.

For now,
I am tired,
my feelings cannot be trusted.

Fatigued brains produce incoherent
thoughts,
and half cooked ideas.

Time to get some sleep.

Small Miracles

It broke!
My chain broke,
and the bead fell to the ground.

What does it mean?

Is there actually a God?
Was this a message?
Was this a test?

My faith in my daughter,
my devotion to her,
my love for her,
all contained in that bead,
just inexplicably fell from my neck.

The chain was not broken,
or pulled.
Later inspection showed,
there was only,
one tiny crack in one link,
and it all came tumbling down.

How did that happen?

I have been having doubts,
I have been having regrets,
I have been pondering the idea,
of leaving her behind.

And now,
my chain breaks,
inexplicably breaks!

Panic,
shock,
disbelief.

What was that?

Was I just tested by God?
Was I just given permission to walk away?

One bead dropping,
just felt like,
the entire cosmos falling down upon me.

Now what do I do?

Stock still I contemplate,
slowly,
a solution arrives.

I fix the chain,
pinch the link closed,
and put the bead back on.

For now,
I carry on.

Drink coffee,
wake my daughter,
and get her to school.

And then,
who knows,
maybe there is another way?

Or maybe,
I can never walk away.

Life So Far

So here I am at almost forty,
unrecognizable to my former self.

I have become a fitness nut.
I wake up at five in the morning,
to workout,
and jog.

I am sober,
dead sober,
a complete and utter teetotaller.

No weed,
no alcohol,
no cigarettes,
coffee my only vice.

I am quasi spiritual,
my former atheist self gapes,
if not cringes at this.

I meditate every day,
and although I still do not believe in god,
I lean towards a greater meaning to life.

— Fractured Thoughts —

I am a father,
I am a husband,
the center of the world to my four year old
daughter.

I am more than my own selfish needs.

My nonchalance has melted away,
replaced by a laser focus,
that I could never have sustained before.

Have I finally found the remote to my brain?
Have I found my new channels?
Maybe,
It is hard to say.

Far too early yet,
for such bold assumptions.

Change is the only constant in life,
I may have the remote today,
but I could still lose it tomorrow.

Perhaps under the couch cushion?

Who knows,
not I.

Here is what I do know.

I like the person that I have become so far,
even if I am more serious,
and have less fun.

I have goals,
ambitions,
targets to meet.

Before I fade away,
there are things that I need say and do.

I sense the urgency now,
the short breath of life.

The privilege of living,
I now know,
is not mine by right.

Clearly I have matured,
but it is more than that.

Some fundamental change has occurred,
that I am only beginning to see play out.

So here is to life so far,
here is to the start of something more.

Change is the only constant in life,
change is a wave,
that I will continue to ride.

ABOUT OKANAGAN PUBLISHING HOUSE

Anyone who has been to the Okanagan knows it is a region of unsurpassed beauty. The splendor of these natural wonders has not been lost on the people who live here. They have provoked many an artist to create works of art.

Okanagan Publishing House is proud to be a small, independent publishing company. We were founded in Vernon, BC and are now based in Kelowna, BC. We began with the desire to showcase the Okanagan, and our focus is on local authors. We work hard to share their stories and art that our beautiful region inspires them to create. And we invite you to experience life with us.

*To learn more about **Okanagan Publishing House**, visit: okanaganpublishinghouse.ca*

Manufactured by Amazon.ca
Bolton, ON

28918939R00070